The No Nonsense Solicitors' Practice: A Guide To Running Your Firm

Bettina Brueggemann,
Solicitor (non-practising),
Management Consultant at Resource7 Ltd,
Commercial Associate at Tenbroeke
Company Ltd

Law Brief Publishing

Published 2017 by
Law Brief Publishing
30 The Parks
Minehead
Somerset
TA24 8BT

www.lawbriefpublishing.com

Paperback: 978-1-911035-25-1

*Dedicated to my Mum and Dad
without whom I would not have
achieved what I have*

Contents

INTRODUCTION

If you are a partner or senior manager in a law firm or legal practice, you will almost certainly have been on courses telling you how to run your firm. The dos and don'ts.

Maybe you have even been given books to read written by some of the leading legal gurus.

In my experience the courses made sense – in theory. Indeed what was said at these courses was certainly not rocket science. And yet the real world is far more complex than these gurus would have you believe.

Although I offer consultancy services I am not a fan of consultants and my advice would be to steer clear of them!

Most will talk in terms of tipping points, how life and your business will follow a pattern if you engage in a certain way and all sorts of consulting speak. There is some merit in everything consultants will tell you but how many of them have had real experience at the coalface? Most I came across have studied business, worked in large organisations and somehow believe that gives them the experience to tell you what you are doing wrong and what you should be doing. Rarely have I seen consultants bring about a change for the better. Rarely have I seen their guidance work. Their only benefit is to challenge you to take a proper look at yourself. Beware however of guidance they offer. Theory is one thing, real life experience of the specific industry another.

Therefore, in this book I do not seek to tell you how to run your firm. Only you will know what works for you.

Instead I invite you to think about my thoughts and observations of running a law firm and form your own conclusions.

My observations are based on 30 years experience at the coal-face, firstly as a practising solicitor, then partner and finally managing partner. In that time there are few situations and circumstances which I did not find myself having to deal with. Whether they related to people, clients, the economic climate, promotion of the firm, development of a business strategy or just general management; my 30 years of working life has been full of challenges. Challenges, which as a qualified solicitor, I had no prior training or experience for. You learn however and you learn quickly.

But my thoughts and observations are not just limited to my own experience. They are also based on having acted for all manner of clients – successful and unsuccessful and learning from them, from their successes and failures. As their lawyer I often guided them not just on the legal issues but also with their strategic decisions, frequently challenging their plans. From them I learnt whether my guidance was right. Often it was but sometimes they were prepared to take risks and assessed situations, quite simply, better than me. This taught me a great deal.

Sometimes I was amazed at their success when their actions flew in the face of experience, logic or common sense. And yet it simply showed that there is no hard and fast rule when it comes to business decisions and running your business. In the end it is what you think and believe that matters, your drive to follow through and your ability to learn from each situation for the future.

When reading this book my hope at one level is that it gives you confidence with questions you may be asking yourself but may not be confident to voice. Maybe some of my observations merely confirm your own thoughts. I hope there will be occasions when you nod and think, "yes I have thought about that", or "it is good to know that at least one other person thinks like I do!"

All law firms are facing challenging times and a constantly changing market. As a profession we have been under scrutiny and attack for years – all in the name of acting in the best interest of the client and "opening up" the market. Our very existence as a profession is and has been under threat and never more so than now.

Hopefully some thought provoking observations will help you work out how best to meet those challenges. You will need to assess for yourself what aspects of what I say you agree with or feel can work for you and which, you feel, should be disregarded or you simply disagree with. At the very least let it challenge your thinking.

Provided you spend real time thinking about your options and approaches and weigh up those options and follow through the chances are you will do well.

CHAPTER ONE
THE NO NONSENSE GUT

The No Nonsense Gut

Although I have not planned the chapters in any kind of order of priority (since I believe they are all equally important) I do find myself placing listening to your gut, or stomach, as I came to call it, top of my list of important lessons to learn when it comes not to just running your business but life in general.

And yet it is not something which in business we talk about much. I would suggest we should.

Listen to your stomach

Some call it emotional intelligence, gut instinct, subconscious or sixth sense. Scientists believe we have two brains – the head brain or conscious brain and the stomach (gut) brain. Research seems to suggest both operate completely separately and independently of each other and that the stomach brain is more powerful or effective. I cannot speak for science but what I did learn over the years was that the times I went wrong was when I failed to listen to my stomach.

Consider when you meet someone for the first time. You may think you assess them based on your conversation, what they say and how they look.

Observe yourself again next time. You might find yourself saying "they seemed quite nice but they are not quite my kind of person", or "I really like them". Your instinct is telling you something additional to your conscious observations.

Sometimes it reinforces your conscious observations leaving you happy and confident with your assessment. Other times it does not and can leave you confused about that "first impression" and the conflict you feel. There is nothing wrong with them, they were perfectly pleasant and yet...

As we are unable to explain the conflict we ignore it relying instead on what we can tangibly relate to, explain and therefore understand. We may simply say "I didn't like them because they said that". The "that" which they said is usually rarely grounds for not liking someone. However as we are unable to explain what we are thinking (and in reality feeling) we may end up simply saying – "I just wasn't keen."

I believe this is your gut instinct at work.

In business and particularly amongst lawyers we never talk about our gut instinct. In fact I think we are often embarrassed to admit that we have a gut instinct particularly if we are not able to explain what we are "feeling" logically and rationally or, worse still for a lawyer and using legal language, at all.

As lawyers we don't deal in feelings. We are trained to analyse and reach conclusions based on information, fact, evidence and our rational and logical analysis of that information and evidence. There is no room for gut instinct.

Our trademark as lawyers is our ability to analyse and think logically. How good we are as lawyers is assessed by how good our analytical and logical skills are. Why would we mention that we also have an instinct? Can you imagine standing up in court and saying "Your Honour my gut instinct in this case is that the defendant is lying and we should not therefore believe him"?

So lawyers ignore it and rarely mention it amongst themselves.

I recall the first time I referred to my stomach telling me something was not a good idea. I saw quizzical expressions pass over faces, polite smiles and immediately lost confidence in my "stomach" and speaking out. I also recall I felt very foolish and naive.

However as the years passed I learnt that whenever I failed to listen to my stomach I made a mistake or a poor decision. This was an important learning curve as the mistakes showed me that my stomach had been right.

Once I realised this and accepted it my gut instinct played a huge role in the decisions I made both professionally and personally. Strange as it may sound not only did it help with the here and now but at times it helped me anticipate what was going to happen in the future.

It may not always be clear but don't ignore your gut

That is not to say that your gut makes it easy for you! Often you may have a feeling but it is hard to interpret it, understand what it is telling you and how you should act on it.

Although it will always be helpful in the end, it may not feel like it at the time. Bear in mind that your gut is talking for a reason – however unclear that might be. For me it became the trigger to take another hard look at the situation and the information available.

I recall being involved in the first interview of quite a senior lawyer. The interview went well. He seemed perfect for the role, had the right experience, seemed pleasant and a cultural fit. And yet something bothered me – a lot. Our HR manager had not picked up on anything and was enthusiastic.

I had no grounds for stopping the recruitment process and so he proceeded to second interview. Instead I asked those carrying out the second interview to "give him a hard time" and really drill down again into his experience, the kind of person he was and just generally. I recall that I kept stressing that they should give him a "hard time" even though I wasn't clear myself what I meant by this. I suppose I wanted them to really check that everything sounded right.

He sailed through the second interview. Everyone was excited. We had been looking for someone like him for quite a long time. There were no grounds for not offering him the job – I was hardly going to persuade colleagues that my stomach had concerns which I could not identify or explain. Despite my confidence in my stomach I was not even sure I could persuade myself!

Our HR department followed the normal procedures for offering a job. However they quickly became concerned when the individual failed to confirm the date they had handed in their notice. Quite a small matter in itself but it was a standard check to help us know when they might roughly be likely to start with us. It also confirmed to us the individual was serious and would not be persuaded to stay where they were. It is not unheard of for candidates to use prospective employers as a bargaining tool for a pay rise from their current employer.

We asked three times but got no reply. Suspicions raised we pursued the question. It transpired that the applicant had already left their previous employment some months earlier. In principle nothing wrong with that either, except that they had not mentioned it at interview. Quite the opposite. They had given the very clear impression that they were still in employment and would need to give 3 months notice. On further investigation it transpired that they had been running a second business alongside their day job, using the firm's contacts and doing work which the firm could have done or would have been interested in getting involved in. Unsurprisingly the firm took exception to this and had dismissed him. Not quite the kind of person we wanted to recruit either.

My gut instinct had been right. I thought back to the interview and it became clear to me what my stomach had picked up on. I was even able to visualise it. His eyes had flickered for a split second uncertainly when I asked what his notice period was. This split second of uncertainty was not someone trying to remember what their notice period was; it was a hesitation before telling a lie. The stomach had understood this whereas the brain had not. The brain had accepted the answer of 3 months notice at face value – the stomach had not.

Take time to reflect

On another occasion I was involved in the recruitment of a senior solicitor – this time for my own department. Again the applicant was highly experienced, had good references, seemed pleasant and intelligent and with good legal skills.

Litigators had been hard to find at the time and we felt we had struck lucky. An offer was made and accepted. Three days after the interview (by which time the offer had been made and accepted) my stomach did summersaults. I was extremely worried. I said to my colleagues that we had made a mistake. We looked at withdrawing the offer but that would not have been very professional and besides which I was unable to explain the reason for my concerns.

The person joined us. From day one they caused problems. It started with them being late on their first day. Never a good sign or start to a new relationship. It continued with them disappearing at noon and returning at 2pm – also on their first day. It was just my luck that the department head was on holiday at the time and it fell to me to deal with the "unusual" behaviour on their first day.

I was told by the employee that they had been looking at cars as they needed to get a new car and had not had time over the weekend. Further he excused his long lunch hour by saying that he did not know what time the firm's lunch hour was – so presumably thought it was in order to take two hours.

Problems continued. As time went by clients complained, he lied about work he had done, deadlines were missed, timesheets were falsified – the list went on. On closer examin-ation it transpired that the references we had received were agreed references and that he had been dismissed from most of his previous employments. In fact we were the last law firm he worked for.

I never understood what it was that I had picked up on or why it took 3 days for the stomach to tell me! It did teach me to listen and delay making offers for a short time. There is a reason why the saying goes "let's sleep on it". Allow the stomach or your subconscious time to work.

Some have a better instinct than others

That is not to say that everyone has a good gut instinct. I know many people who have a poor instinct. I do not know why that might be but having said that I doubt there is anyone who has no instinct at all. It is a basic animal skill which humans have not lost completely but is of course not as prevalent as with animals. I believe that through experience and a greater understanding of how it works it is possible to develop it.

Can you persuade others to rely on it? Why should they rely on your instinct particularly if theirs is saying something different?

That is a very fair question but remember this is not a contest. I have never tried to understand the instinct of others. You can't. Equally do not assume that your instinct will pick up on everything. It will not and cannot. On that basis and if you find yourself disagreeing with a colleague about your "instincts" the chances are that neither of you are wrong. What is more likely to be the case is that you have picked up on different things. Listen to what you are both thinking and it might be that between you, you get a more rounded and complete picture of the situation.

Therefore, whether we accept it, consciously or subconsciously, your stomach, your gut instinct, your subconscious plays a part in the decisions you reach and how you act.

A great deal can still be logically analysed and rationalised with the brain. I do not seek to undervalue the conscious brain and its ability to assess situations. My point is do not ignore your gut instinct if it raises its head. Take time to rethink what you are planning to do. Reassess all the information you have and look again at everything more carefully. Keep at the back of your mind something might be afoot, not quite right or just not the right thing to do. Try to work out what it might be. There is a reason why your stomach is talking to you even if the message is unclear confusing or even seems stupid.

Look at your gut instinct as simply another tool you have that can help you make the best decisions. It is a complicated tool, it can take time to understand and sometimes you may not be able to. You can however learn from it. Above all don't ignore it and allow it to play a part in your decision making process.

CHAPTER TWO
THE NO NONSENSE SHEEP

Who are we?

We lawyers are a strange lot aren't we? We recognise each other quite easily. I am not sure why or how that is, maybe it has something to do with how we talk, walk and behave. Maybe this is true of all professions and each profession recognises it has unique and, in the main, defined characteristics. After all each type of work will attract a certain kind of person and perhaps we should not therefore be surprised to find a level of similarity amongst those of us doing similar work.

For example litigators attract a different type of personality to those who do conveyancing or wills and trusts. Indeed I recall being told that "we litigators" were aggressive. We never saw ourselves like that. Maybe in hindsight and compared to the more placid and gentle conveyancers and probate lawyers we probably do have more aggressive tendencies and our approach is generally more confrontational.

When it comes to lawyers we tend to be solo players. Our teams may consist of our secretary and our client (but we really do not like clients interfering too much) and depending on the type of law you practice some experts such as barristers or other specialists. I do not mean to suggest that lawyers do not or cannot work in large teams but as partners and senior lawyers we frequently work alone or with individuals to whom we give instructions.

We have to rely on ourselves and our analysis and we give guidance and advice on which our clients rely. We carry quite a lot of responsibility as leaders of our teams and although our clients make the decisions (and we are always very careful to ensure that is the case as we do not like risk) they do so based on what we tell them. We see ourselves as individuals rather than team players who like to do things the way we want. We do not like procedural restrictions and given the choice we like to be mavericks. We are individuals. Tough characteristics in an environment of greater and greater bureaucracy.

Although I mention these characteristics a little tongue in cheek and with an element of exaggeration there is nevertheless a lot of truth in the description. Even if one takes them as semi valid characteristics you would think that we would run our law firms on an individual basis too.

Not so. I have always been amazed by how law firms follow the trend. In the same way that I do not understand why youngsters pay a lot of money for torn jeans simply because it is the fashion (I tend to throw away my clothes that are torn) I do not understand why lawyers are keen to follow a trend simply because everyone says it is a good thing to do. I suppose conversely you could ask why would you expect lawyers to act differently to most of mankind?

I do not want to be philosophical but have always asked the question – "is it because human beings are in principle sheep?"

One person does something and if it gets enough attention everyone else follows? I fear that is probably the case and maybe entrepreneurs who are successful are successful in part because they are prepared to buck the trend, think outside the box and go it alone against popular thinking.

Avoid trends

Some trends and approaches are good and make sense and are good to follow but only if you have truly analysed the trend and it is the right approach for your firm. Trends are guidelines not to be followed no matter what.

Over 20 years ago it became the mantra amongst law firm consultant gurus that law firms had to change. Change and managing change were "in words". Indeed one colleague I worked with constantly referred to the fact that we had to change. When I asked him in what way he was unable to say – just that we had to change.

What disturbed me at the time was not the fact that we should change but that the driver was outside "fashion" rather than an understanding of the market, how it was chan-ging and the fact that what we were doing might not meet that challenging market and it was for that reason that we had to change.

The trouble with following a trend is that you may be chan-ging things for the sake of change and not because it improves the delivery of your service, the business as a whole or certain aspects of it. Change for the sake of change is to my mind never worthwhile. Quite the opposite. It is disruptive, destabilising and can be very damaging.

An observation I made very early on in my career was how new bosses make changes very quickly after taking on their new role. Even as a young inexperienced lawyer I never understood how someone taking over a new team understood what changes were good to make so soon after taking office. For a while I thought they had to be very clever. That was until I saw that the changes were often a reversal of what the previous incumbent in post had done.

For a few years we used to have a partnership secretary (another popular trend which all law firms were supposed to have but which thinking now seems largely to have been abandoned) whose responsibility in part was to manage the finance team. When the first partnership secretary was appointed our finance team was spread out amongst a number of offices. Within a few weeks the decision was taken that you had to centralise the team as this would work better. Huge change while people moved around, big disruptions in all offices.

One or two years later when a new partnership secretary was appointed the decision, again taken within a few weeks, was that the finance team should be decentralised and spread out amongst the offices. It would mean offices would get better finance support by having people physically present in their office. Huge change while people moved around, big disruption to all offices. I won't even mention the actual cost involved of setting up new work stations, HR time and work time disruption on both occasions.

What I observed through this time was that the actual working of the department was not looked at nor were the people in the department asked for their views. How did they think it worked, what did they think was working and what was not. How did they think things could be improved? So I came to the conclusion that this "change" was a sign of control, showing the partners that "they were doing something" and a means of putting their stamp on their new role. The changes had little to do with achieving any benefit or improvement for the department or for the firm and indeed neither change created a particular improvement.

Be careful about change for the sake of change

Change for the sake of change is not usually a good thing but change which improves things is – obvious really. So why is it that businesses and law firms often make changes for no reason other than that it is modern way of doing it?

About 15 years ago it became the "thing to do" for law firms to convert to LLP. The guideline was that the change would take about 12–16 months and costs would be considerable – new headed paper, new signs, probably a new branding.

Arguments for were that it would limit your liability as partners, made you more corporate and modern.

I was never persuaded. Indeed I used to argue why stop at the half way house – why not go the whole way and become limited.

If you wanted to limit your liability, a limited company achieved that far more than an LLP. If you wanted to develop a corporate structure a limited company gave you that far more than an LLP. As far as the public was concerned personal liability offered by partners versus limiting your liability to them under an LLP never seemed a very strong selling point to me.

I always remained unpersuaded that the cost and manpower needed to effect this change justified the benefit of such a change – particularly as I was hard pressed to identify a tangible benefit in the first place.

I used to argue that if liability was the concern you would be better placed to increase your insurance cover.

As time went by this became more relevant when it transpired that under an LLP as a member you were solely liable for your errors (as opposed to the members as a whole) and that you needed to put in place individual insurance (as well as LLP insurance) and agree with your fellow members that liability was joint and several – all of which of course is already the case within a partnership.

If taking out bank loans, banks still required personal guarantees from the members and the same tended to apply for mainstream investment. The ability to limit your liability was severely restricted.

If introducing a corporate style structure was the goal then I argued why not just set that up within the partnership and see how it worked. Why go through the expensive process of conversion when the people and behaviours were likely to remain the same.

Indeed many firms who converted to LLP simply continued to manage themselves as they had as a partnership and went so far as to continue to refer to themselves as partners.

Changing your name or legal entity does not change how you operate. This will only happen if you change your behaviours.

In an environment where time is a premium and there are rarely enough hours in the day to get everything done you need to choose your projects carefully and work on those that give you genuine rewards as opposed to just following a trend. Converting to an LLP to my mind did not make you a better law firm, delivering a better service. All it did was cost a lot of money without delivering a return. I always felt I had more important worthwhile projects to spend my time on and rejected conversion simply because everyone else was doing it and it was the modern way of doing things.

Think individually and be individuals

Many law firms went straight to redundancies in the 2008 crash. In fact most businesses did. It is what business does when there is a sharp downturn of work. I wonder for how many this was a knee jerk reaction vindicated by the fact that everyone else was doing it?

It was of course my first thought too. I was on holiday in America when the Lehman Brothers crash occurred. As soon as I heard about it on the news I knew that this downturn would take many years to recover from. I am not an economist but my gut instinct told me at the time that this was big and we would not recover quickly.

I also recognised that we needed to react quickly but as for everyone the question was how and in what way. Everyone else was making redundancies and so the action which could be least criticised was to follow that trend. However as a non believer in trends and that you should think about options yourself I came to a different conclusion.

Although some colleagues wanted to, we avoided redundancies. Instead we reduced the days worked by all staff thereby retaining them all but reducing overheads.

I am not seeking to argue that that was the right decision. That is a matter for hindsight but that is not the point. The question is more whether businesses looked at all options, where they as a firm were, their future plans and whether they concluded that redundancies were the best option in all the circumstances.

The fact that law firms in our area were all making redundancies (and changed this approach only much later) makes me ask the question "did they just follow what everyone else was doing?"

Surely we cannot have been the only law firm who thought it would be more beneficial to look after our staff, not lose good people, and put ourselves in a position to meet demand when the upturn happened, while at the same time avoiding expensive redundancy payments (at a time when you can least afford them) and reducing overheads with virtual immediate effect?

Change is good. The old adage that minor changes can increase productivity I believe has a lot of merit. Some changes can be uplifting and encourage your staff, show that you are staying ahead of the game or that you are investing in your firm – that you are not "old". My point is be independent and think independently about what change is right for you.

Just because everyone else is doing it does not makes it right or a good decision for your firm. Will the change create a tangible benefit? Can you identify it and can you measure it? What do you expect from this change? Is it worthwhile given everything else you have to do? Do it because you believe it has merit, don't do it because everyone else is and don't do it for the sake of change.

CHAPTER THREE
NO NONSENSE LOOKING
AFTER YOUR PENNIES

I don't know why it is but lawyers seem to have an inherent difficulty when it comes to thinking about finances and money. Maybe the next generation of lawyers will be different as our profession becomes more business-like. I hope so.

Be commercial

Throughout my working life I was repeatedly astounded by the lack of commerciality I encountered amongst lawyers. And I mean all lawyers, juniors, partners and senior managers. This in my experience seems to be a universal problem in law firms and one which you rarely come across in accountancy firms. Accountants look at lawyers with awe and a complete lack of understanding when it comes to their financial abilities.

I frequently discussed this with other managing partners and we were universal in our criticism of lawyers. Lawyers seem to have an issue when it comes to money.

"My client can't pay but I can't abandon them", "I know he owes us £30k and he has not paid the last 3 bills but he will pay so I need to continue to work for them", "why do we not pay all our bills on time", "I am embarrassed to ask for monies on account".

These were universal statements fellow managing partners complained about as excuses given by their lawyers.

In contrast when I had works done at home the plumber confirmed he could do the work but said "I can do it but you know time is money."

What is it about lawyers that we have such an issue with money, asking for it or ensuring that clients pay us? And not only does this affect how we treat our clients but it also seems to translate itself into the financial management of law firms. Somehow we always seem to think it will sort itself out and we can turn a blind eye to our finances.

Managing the firm's finances is not rocket science. Hopefully most of us manage our finances at home sensibly. We earn money and we have outgoings. We try not to spend more than we earn. If you do, over time, you get into financial difficulties. Sometimes as an investment or as part of a larger plan we borrow money – in order to buy our house for example. We then pay it off over time. Why should business be any different? The numbers are bigger, the principles the same.

When we buy a washing machine or some clothes we expect to pay for them there and then. We do not expect the shop to give us credit. Our credit card might but not the shop.

Have respect for yourself

Why do we think it is in order for our clients to treat us differently to how they buy other items? Is it because deep down we feel we cannot justify our fees? If so as a profession we need to rethink our charges but until then we nevertheless need to act in a commercial way to ensure that our business is paid for the work we do.

Income - Expenditure = profit

And yet lawyers seem unable to do that and somehow act differently when it comes to their business? Why are lawyers unable to reconcile the fact that income and outgoings represent profit, that generating income enables wages to be paid and that the need to ensure a healthy cash flow is essential for future efficient running of the business and its survival?

Sadly, during my many years of acting for clients I saw some good businesses fail not because the core nature of the business was flawed (indeed some were very good and successful as a concept) but because the owners had no idea of how to manage their finances. By the time I saw them it was often too late but had they paid more attention to the financial side of the business while they had the chance their actual core business could have made them very rich. Instead they faced bankruptcy.

I also came across law firms who never reviewed their outgoings and paid little attention to the level of their income and debtor levels, and then wondered why they made so little profit. Occasionally I came across law firms who kept a tight rein on their outgoings, set clear defined targets, made sure they were achieved, made sure clients paid and earnt very well. I spent a lot more time talking to them!

The annual budget is important

The annual budget should be your key to setting yourself up for the next year and should represent the effective financial management of your firm. It is a kind of reference book, which can be adapted, adjusted but is the guide and measure of how well you are doing and should act as a control of your finances.

Seen perhaps as a pain or a nuisance to prepare, if you believe in its usefulness and as the process which most challenges where you are and where you want to be and how to get there, the "chore" becomes a vital part of you running a successful firm.

Your annual budget does three things.

Firstly it forces you to review your expenditure. Is it justified, can it be reduced, is how you are spending your money supporting the plans you have set for your business, is it excessive, are you getting any benefit from your spending, what are you planning on doing over the next year, how much will that cost and looking at the whole picture does it still stack up as worthwhile?

It is a health check and should force you to take time to rethink what you are doing, to challenge your plans and check the viability of the financial aspect of your business and your plans.

Secondly it challenges you to identify what income you need to allow for this expenditure and generate a profit acceptable to you.

Thirdly and finally having forced you to address the first two points it then forces you to identify how you are going to achieve the income needed to deliver everything that the budget provides for.

It is easy to say you want to earn £x but how are you going to do it?

As part of this process you may chose to budget for a reduced profit for one or more years as part of a planned investment strategy which you believe will ultimately lead to higher profits and a better business in the long term. There is nothing wrong with this provided it is a conscious decision by all the partners with full knowledge and understanding of the consequences both for them, the business and the staff.

If this is not the case and you don't like the results of your income/expenditure budget it is time to go back to the drawing board, revisit your plans and aspirations and income generation and possibly your whole business model.

I recall many discussions about how the profit was not where it should be, agreed by all the partners and leading to the realisation that income needed to be improved. However then, when discussing expenditure I found the partners wanting to increase the expenditure because "we must do this and we must do that". No matter how much I stressed we were going in the wrong direction and that instead of reducing expenditure to improve profit we were increasing it and thereby decreasing the already insufficient profit, my comments tended to fall on deaf ears. Then sometimes a little while later would come the sudden realisation that we were not making enough profit!

Although disheartening at the time they were in the long term useful discussions. It was only by repeatedly highlighting the issues and having the discussions that the lack of commerciality amongst some partners came to light and started the process of getting them to think more commercially. The discussions were the start of tackling the problem.

However, lawyers need to move on between this disconnect between income and expenditure and understand fully the effect on profit. It isn't rocket science just simple maths.

Tackle the thorny subject of targets

Setting your projected income on the other hand is a challenge for all law firms and always has been. How should you set your targets for your lawyers? Interestingly it does not appear to be a challenge for accountants. They are very clear about how they calculate targets and what they expect of their staff and it is usually a lot tougher than the expectations in law firms.

I have known a few businesses to argue that simply by delivering an exceptional service the income generates itself. Personally whereas I think this idea could work for a boutique business, in general I doubt it can succeed amongst lawyers. It would be a brave law firm indeed that approaches its income generation on that basis for the simple reason that even this approach requires a good commercial approach and financial acumen.

Allowing your client to decide how much to pay you is another concept which has over time been mooted. I have to say I liked it as a concept. It certainly is outside the box of how lawyers operate.

Its success is based on the argument that clients often over-value the work and pay more than you would have charged. Would I have ever had the courage to implement this? Probably not. I am not a big enough entrepreneur!

It could perhaps work for wills and conveyancing but litigation which goes on for years might be more challenging. I would however love to see a firm try this. Don't be fooled however. A good financial acumen is still essential if it were to work successfully. You could not just let it run itself and hope that somehow the figures would stack up. Your staff would need to be financially astute and on the ball. Sitting behind even this concept would need to be a clear understanding of how much you would expect your staff to generate, how much you need to generate and a constant monitoring of the position.

If the more innovative ideas are not an option then a look at more traditional approaches would seem to be the answer.

When I started out in the law you were supposed to achieve 3 times your salary. Back then I used to question the evidential basis for this. The answer always given was one third salary, one third overheads and one third profits. Somehow no one was ever able to provide a proper financial calculation to support this however – it was just accepted as the basis of setting targets because that was how it had always been done.

As the years passed, although some stuck stubbornly to the 3 times salary concept there began to be talk of a 4 times salary target. Law firms now had marketing and IT costs which had not been the case in the past. Still however, no calculations to support this concept.

How is it that a profession as old as the legal profession works on a concept, which at some point someone, many years ago, came up with (perhaps based on some logic), and follows it blindly for years without question and without testing its validity and viability? Where is our independence of thought?

There was a time when my firm looked at "what did you achieve last year" and increased it a little. After all if you only achieved £50k last year how can you achieve much more next? It was not an uncommon approach in those days for many firms.

It was, however, a very poor basis for setting targets and one which for us over the years caused a decline in the performance and profitability of the firm. Those that underperformed got rewarded with a lower target and those who performed well were rewarded with an even higher target. Not a good motivator and the reality was that as the years passed the performance of most fee earners simply declined.

When I looked at it from my firm's perspective I rejected the 4 times salary target. It worked for lawyers on higher salaries but not for more junior staff and therefore across the firm as a whole. It seemed to me that there was no direct relationship between the salary paid and the basis on which our staff were charged out to the client. Nor did it take account of the kind of return we should have expected given the hours worked and the charge out rate.

Set fair but tough and challenging targets

Going back to basics – what is it we actually do?

We sell time and we do so by the hour and in units of 6. We work a 7 hour day, 5 days a week. We have 5 or 6 weeks holiday and 8 bank holidays. We might on average be sick for a week.

The Law Society says that we should expect fee earners to work 1200 hours a year – taking into account the above. Many firms require in excess of this. However taking this as the guideline this worked out on average to 4.5 chargeable hours per day. If one applied the unit rate it represented less than 4.5 chargeable hours a day. In other words you could chat and deal with administration for in excess of 2 hours a day.

This didn't seem unreasonable. Since we charge out our fee earners at an hourly rate the starting point for a target ought to be the number of hours we expect our lawyers to work (daily, weekly, monthly, yearly) multiplied by the hourly rate.

Needless to say this approach produced shock and horror not just amongst the staff but also partners and I have to confess me. It produced materially higher targets than had ever been set before. Some staff found their targets increasing from the low figures of £70,000 to £180,000 and higher.

It also put us in the right direction to identifying the sort of income we needed to generate to develop the business in line with our plans and produce a profit more in line with our expectations.

Given the reaction some allowances seemed appropriate. It was unlikely that a fee earner would recover the entire hourly rate 100% of the time. Clients complain and want reductions. There are always some write offs. Therefore I deducted 10% off the target to allow for credits, discounts write offs and the like.

I argued that you could of course give a bigger discount to the hourly rate but if the discount was too high that in turn raised a number of questions.

If it was true that on average we only recovered 70% or even 50% of our hourly rate in a department or for a particular fee earner this had to mean that either

(a) the hourly rate was too high, in which case we should reduce it (afterall why tell a client we are charging a higher hourly rate than what we will actually charge at the end of the day –you might as well take the competitive advantage and enjoy the benefit, in the client's eyes, of charging a lower rate at the outset); or

(b) the work is not feasible at the rate we want to charge it out at and might not be worth doing; or

(c) you need to review how the fee earner undertakes the work.

The reason for why a Will that should take 3 hours to prepare but which takes a particular fee earner 7 hours needs to be explored.

Equally, in reality only being able to charge £100 per hour for work you actually thought you were charging out at £200 per hour must at least put into question the viability of undertaking that work in the first place. It might be that £100 per hour will still generate a healthy profit. You need to know this however to enable you to make informed decisions.

Target setting can have consequences

When we implemented this target setting it was not without consequences. We discovered that one area of the firm was operating at a loss which could not be sustained long term. None of us had ever understood this to be the case. Indeed we had thought the opposite, namely that it was very profitable. Tough decisions and a parting of the ways ensued.

There was one fee earner who had been with us for a long time who was outraged about the fact that we were asking them to do 4 chargeable hours a day. They felt that 2 hours (which is what they had been achieving) was adequate. He asked to be made redundant. I suggested he look for another job. Let him drag another firm down – but not us any longer was my thinking.

I am not suggesting that this approach to setting targets is the right one. There are lots of variations and alternatives. Indeed in an environment where there is a greater demand for fixed fees a different approach might be appropriate.

However even with fixed fees there needs to be a starting basis for setting the fixed fee. Most likely it will be based on the estimated time needed to complete the work and the cost of doing the work with profit included. Time and cost will therefore always play a role much as it does in all lines of work.

It is a thorny subject but if you take a proper and commercial approach be alive to the fact that, as it did for us it, there might be some curve balls. You may be in for some surprises good and bad, and perhaps tough decisions. Avoiding the issue however merely puts off the difficult day.

Setting your targets is a key element of preparing your budget and developing your business strategy. It underpins your income, your ability to meet your overheads, the generation of your profit and your ability to implement your strategic plans.

Be able to explain how you set your targets

Bear in mind there is no perfect method for setting targets and every firm needs to adapt its approach to match the kind of firm they are. Key is the ability to explain the basis on which targets are set to staff and to be able to show that there is merit and justification for how they are calculated. This will then enable you to challenge underperformance.

For us it did achieve over time a material increase in perform-ance. It was not without a lot of hard work, discussion and consequences. However it was an essential process for the business to work through in order to be able to develop and move forward. The benefit of tackling it was that it enabled us to be proactive rather than reactive. We chose to make changes before circumstances forced us to and thereby took control.

So, expenditure and targets are set and you now know what income you are looking to achieve. Hopefully it is ambitious and stretching but achievable bar disasters. Do you put your budget away and get on with life as normal. In the good old days that is precisely what you used to do. No more.

Sleep with your budget by your side

Close monitoring of all aspects of your budget remains a key element of running a successful law firm. If performance is not being achieved you might need to react quickly. You cannot allow your expenditure to continue as planned if you are not achieving the required income.

Review write-offs and question why they are happening. Review time recorded and question if the required chargeable hours are not being achieved individually and across the firm. Without them you cannot achieve your projected income.

Monitoring performance on all levels is key to maintaining your budget.

Cash is king

But it does not stop there. Cash flow is as important as your budget. In fact at one level it can be more important. Running out of money could be the end of your business. Ensure you have a good understanding of your cash flow and how this will look over the next few months.

Put in place proper credit control.

Review the amount of credit you offer any one client. Consider setting credit limits for clients you do a lot of work for but who are slow payers. Do not expose yourself too much to any one client.

Most litigators will have come across at least one case where their client was owed an amount of money they simply could not afford to lose. When it happened to a very established client of mine who had been in business for many years it was a salutary lesson to him and me. When he came to me he was owed over £50k (worth more then, than now) by one client who had gone into liquidation. My client was distraught. He did not think he could survive this loss. His business was not huge and it represented too large a loss to overcome. Having nothing to lose we went to court seeking an injunction preventing sale of the goods which included parts we had provided but not been paid for. We argued retention of title.

Put under pressure the liquidators finally agreed to pay £44k plus costs (but only after we have obtained an injunction). It saved the client's business. It taught me how quickly things can turn around.

Effective credit control means good cash flow. It also highlights danger situations and exposures which as a business owner you might not otherwise pick up on by other means. A good credit control is worth its weight in gold.

Understand profit is not cash

And so it brings me to a further disconnect that lawyers suffer from – the difference between cash and profit. Unfortunately profit is not cash. Your monthly profit and loss account might show you have generated a healthy profit but that does not mean you can have it paid out to you. Why? Profit is not cash. Profit on paper does not mean your clients have paid you and that you have that profit in the bank. You need to be paid before you can have your profit.

Is it all about finance?

Do finances sit at the core of a business' success? In reality the success depends on many factors and as they are all interlinked you cannot say in isolation that one will determine its success without the others. It is a chicken and egg scenario. However without money and the ability to pay wages and outgoings a business can go nowhere and indeed cannot survive – even if all other elements are good.

Consultants tell you that if you get the service right the money follows. I don't agree. It is a "make you feel good statement" but rarely true. A good business without good financial management does not survive. You can be doing very good business but if your clients are not paying you or you are not charging enough, you will not survive long term.

Without good financial management I believe most businesses are likely, in the end, to encounter difficulties. It might take time and a business can limp along but eventually there are likely to be problems.

I apologise for criticising lawyers in the way I have. There are, of course lawyers who are great at financial management. Indeed, much of what I have said here is obvious and is certainly not novel thinking, and yet it is a battle I encountered time and time again and was the main complaint of other managing partners. Maybe as lawyers we do understand but are just not good at implementation. Whatever the reason, my observations are far more common that one might think.

Shall I be conservative or adventurous

My final comment on financial management is to ponder which is best – a conservative approach or adventurous approach.

Quite frankly I never worked out the answer and I used to repeatedly challenge my thinking here. Personally I always took a more conservative approach to the financial management of the firm. In part this sits more comfortably with lawyers as we are a conservative breed and suggesting radical new approaches and thinking is likely to be too hard to push past your partners. We are not great risk takers.

I believed in a strong cash base from which to operate. I was against overdraft as a matter of operating the business and it was the first thing I reversed. Some of my partners at times expressed the view that we should operate on overdraft but I never understood the logic of working on overdraft as a matter of principle. It is expensive and gives you no buffer in times of a downturn. Indeed when the 2008 crash happened we were grateful to have been cash rich without overdraft. It enabled us to survive the downturn with a level of confidence that I know many other law firms did not have.

Equally I do believe that overdrafts and loans have their place. It seems to me, however, that there needs to be a purpose for working on overdraft and it should be part of a specific plan as opposed to because the business is not generating enough cash to sustain itself. If the business is not generating sufficient cash to sustain itself it is time to take a hard look at how you operate and revise your overall strategy – not at overdrafts.

Investing in the business with the benefit of overdraft or loans is often essential to implement strategic decisions and provided these are thought through and part of a clear plan have every chance of supporting the success of the firm.

At the same time – no risk no gain. Also true. A conservative approach is not always the best either. It can stop you taking up opportunities which might only come along once in a while. It can stop you taking chances. If you want to succeed you have to take chances, at some point.

For that reason it is impossible to say which is the best approach. Timing can be a huge factor. Those who invested in their firm in 2007 came unstuck in 2008. They could not have foreseen what would happen and had the crash not happened their investment would probably have worked well for them. As it is and as we know some large law firms collapsed.

In the end we can only do our best with the information we have. What is important is that there is proper financial management of the firm and a full understanding of the financial position of the firm at all times. Always think through your approach carefully and the reasons for doing so. Make sure that they stand up to scrutiny and challenge and that they are moving you forward in the direction you believe it is right for you to go.

CHAPTER FOUR
NO NONSENSE FUTURE

Every consultant and business advisor will tell you that you must have a business plan. The idea is as old as business itself. When I became a partner we spent months preparing our business plan. In the end it was professionally bound and took the form of a book. It must have been at least 50 pages long. Once finished it sat on a shelf and was never referred to again. As it was prepared on the basis of a 5 year plan it was an excuse not to have to prepare another plan for a few years. After all we had a business plan.

I recall that when we did revisit it on one rare occasion we saw that the plan had been to reduce one of our departments and move away from legal aid work. At the time the plan was written, there were about 9 fee earners in the department. At the time of our revisit a few years later, having removed the dust, instead of reducing the head count in that department it had risen to 16 and we were doing more legal aid work than ever. How did this happen? We had a business plan.

Keep your business plan short

I believe a business plan should be no more than 2 pages long (and if possible just one page). You might want to have a longer document setting out your thinking and the basis on which you have developed your summary but the driver and reference document needs to be short clear and concise as to its objectives. 50 pages of script is not a concise plan. It is something designed to put you to sleep.

There is no doubt that preparing your plan for your business is an extremely hard and difficult exercise. If you do not live and breathe your plan it **will not** happen. If you do not know what your plan is it **cannot** happen.

It requires a true and honest understanding of your business , who you are, your objectives and what your real business is about and what you all want.

What kind of a law firm are you? Are you a boutique or general practice? Are you cheap and pile them high or expensive offering, quality. Can quality only be delivered at a more expensive price or is there a compromise? What do you mean by quality and how does this differentiate between those offering the same service at a lower price. What do you offer that is different? Where do you see the future market lie and how do you propose to tap into it or retain it depending on where you are?

The list of questions that you need to put to yourself are deep and probing. If answered properly they will give you a picture of the type of plan you should be developing and how you should go about it.

Consultants are happy to spend days with you helping you work this out – but in my experience it has very rarely lead to any real changes or better understanding let alone an effective business plan.

Really challenge your objectives

One, and it is only one, of the reasons for this I came to believe, is that there is a fundamental question that is not explored as deeply as it should be, if at all. Maybe this is because it might show a divide in the partnership, it might have serious consequences for the partnership and it might throw the entire business on its head.

What do you as owners want out of the business?

When you start out in your career you might want to be part of something that is growing and have the romantic notion of having been part of building an "empire". Leaving something behind when you are pushing up the daisies. Leaving a legacy. With an old established firm, making sure the firm continues after you are gone for the next generation.

Of course you want to earn well in the meantime but there is another driver which is not purely financial. Lawyers can be quite romantic!

As you get older this might become less important. Ensuring that you are financially secure and achieving a good financial exit can become greater drivers.

Alternatively you might just want to make as much money as possible and retire and close the business. I recall meeting a branding consultant who had set up his business some 7 years earlier and was doing very well. He was driven purely by money and he made no bones about it. His motive was not about leaving anything behind. Make as much money as possible and then get out, by sale or otherwise was his moto.

Maybe the driver is to help people and making money is secondary. You want to live yes but wealth is not as important.

If you are entering the arena of alternative business structures with a view to introducing financial investors they will have clear objectives and they will rarely have anything to do with leaving a legacy or helping people! It will be about financial return and profit.

Thinking back to when I started out, it was about making the business bigger and better and leaving something behind. I recall many discussions with contemporaries (not just in the law) and many had big plans for their business. Maybe life grinds you down but those with big plans when in their 30s and who are now in their 50s are now much more focused on making their money and then either selling up or closing their business when they are ready to retire. Their priority is setting themselves up for retirement and enjoying the work they are doing in the meantime. Earning and reducing the stress (rather than increasing it which comes with expansion and big plans) are now bigger drivers.

The age difference alone can therefore create a conflict or at least a difference in objectives between partners. It is not irreconcilable but acknowledging them and working with them when identifying overall what you want out of the business is key to then setting out your business plan.

Who are you, take your head out of the sand?

In the backdrop of your objectives what kind of a law firm are you or do you want to be? Where do you see the market going and what are your clients' expectations going to be now and in the future? The legal landscape is changing at an unprecedented pace. It is a frightening place and, if you are a generalist firm, it can be difficult to know what might be for the best.

However the fact that it is difficult does not mean putting your head in the sand is a good idea. Of course you can only do your best given all the information and where you are. Doing nothing however should not be an option.

How do you want to offer your service and what use should you make of technology. There is no doubt that technology must play a part in your offering but to what extent?

If you want to deliver quality what do you mean by this and how do you define it. What do you do that is extra or different and better to the law firm down the road or the law firm offering services online or in the north at a fraction of the price?

Quality is such an overused word and every business says this is what they offer. If that is right why, apparently, are so many clients unhappy with their lawyers and why does the legal profession appear to have such a poor reputation – which I hasten to say I feel is in many ways unjustified?

We all have different expectations of quality and I suspect this is what makes it so hard to deliver. However when it is delivered you know. We all know.

When I had an extension done it was for the purpose of adding an en-suite. All building works are stressful and even more so when you have a busy job. As expected there were the unexpected problems, some small some bigger. The plumber was excellent and the reason was he resolved them all even when they did not relate to the plumbing work he was doing. It included picking up the plaster boards for the tiler and even fixing a door handle on the airing cupboard. Now that really had nothing to do with the works at all. Small things, inexpensive things but I found myself saying that whatever he was going to charge he was worth it.

I tried to analyse my reaction and I came to the conclusion that he took away the problems and gave me confidence to rely on him. I did not have to think about the ongoing works and was able to trust him to sort everything out. He was simply excellent – and he was not cheap!

I came to the conclusion that although everyone has their own standards of quality it tends to have something to do with removing the worry, trust and reliance.

If as a law firm one can achieve that feeling in all clients (they are worth it whatever they charge) you have probably cracked quality service.

Equally cheap and not delivering top quality has its place in the market. There are plenty of shops who do not pretend to offer quality goods. Their goods might only last a summer but they are cheap. You do not expect anything else and if they last longer you are impressed.

Are you about value for money or do you offer something extra and if so what is it.

Don't pretend to be what you are not

Whatever the offering and the basis of delivery be clear about it. Don't pretend to be something you are not. If you are in one place but want to get somewhere else your business plan needs to set out how you are going to achieve it, your times-cale and what needs to be done. Don't pretend you have already got there.

Think carefully about expansion

What about expansion? Is this part of your plan? If so – into new areas of law, existing areas, locations, or complementary fields or mergers?

We have over the last decade seen many mergers. Some have worked, some have not. Of course it depends on where you sit in the merger. Those that don't move with the merger or are let go a year later might say it has not worked – for them at least. Some have very publicly simply imploded.

In the 80s some law firms branched out into estate agencies. Those local to us failed. Law firms then acquired financial services arms to complement the trust departments. Most have sold them off. Accountants are keen to have a legal arm. It has spelled disaster for some accountancy firms. As a result of ABS options I suspect we are likely to see more mergers between accountants, surveyors and law firms. In theory they complement each other. There is without a doubt in terms of a client's overall need a synergy.

I would encourage caution. Not because I do not think it can work. Far from it. If approached in the right way it can work. The fundamental issue is the difference in ethos and culture that different types of business attract. Accountants are very commercial in their overall approach. They would struggle with the lack of commerciality amongst lawyers. Estate agents are very different in their whole work practices to lawyers. Seeking to impose lawyer ethos and mentality on estate agents simply would not work.

I do wonder however that lawyers who struggle to make their own businesses efficient and successful think they can understand another business and make it successful – because both those aspects would be key to its success. You need to understand a business to make it successful.

Be very clear about the reason for the expansion. Growth for the sake of growth is not necessarily a good thing. My father had a very astute friend who was also extremely successful in business. He gave me some advice very early on which I always bore in mind. He said that if you want to grow your business you need to understand that there comes a point at which you need to go seriously big. Every business has an optimal size at which it runs economically and profitably. If you do not go big after reaching your optimal size you simply increase overheads but do not increase profit and eventually start going backwards. Knowing when to go big might be hard to assess but it is something to bear in mind if you have expansion plans.

Stick to what you are good at and have a clear plan

At an annual conference I hosted over 10 years ago I had arranged for someone from Philips to speak. Two points have stayed with me. The first was that although a much bigger business with £00 on their balance sheets that would make your head spin, the issues he described on all aspects of running the business were the same as we were facing at the time. Different business, same issues. It was a great comfort.

Secondly he described how they had for years encouraged innovation and supported new ideas. This meant they had allowed new ideas free reign and ventured into different areas as a result. When business took a downturn and they were forced to take a long hard look at themselves they discovered that they were building aeroplane engines and things which were not at the core of their business. I recall him saying "what did we really know about building aeroplane engines. Our expertise was in TV and electronics. We decided to go back to what we knew and were good at and build on that ".

I thought it was a salutary lesson, not against diversification but against diversification without clear thought and a plan for branching out in the first place.

Your plans for your business should therefore encompass what you as owners want to get out of it, why you as individuals are in business, what type of business you are, what are you actually offering, what your plans for the future are and how that will be achieved.

Get that onto two pages and you have a clear plan.

Be efficient

A final word on efficiencies which need to appear in your plans for the future. Another hard fact of life but there is a constant drive for more for less. We are all guilty of this and must all take the blame for this shift in culture. We expect the same service and quality at an ever decreasing cost. We all want more for less.

Efficiencies require change in work practices and better use of IT – Something which can be hard to achieve in a profession which dislikes change. However ignore at your peril. Everyone can work smarter and more efficiently and it does not have to come at the cost of quality.

CHAPTER FIVE
NO NONSENSE YOU ARE
THE BIG CHEESE

As owners of the business you are leaders whether you like it or not and whether you are good at it or not. Accept therefore that you are a leader.

You may have a managing partner who leads on a day to day basis but staff will nevertheless look to all partners or members for leadership. They will expect you collectively and as individuals to set the standards, give guidance and above all set the example.

I believe good leaders are rare. The world would be a far better place if we had more true leaders. Sadly we are all dogged by personal needs and characteristics which interfere with good leadership. Whether it is because we have an inherent need to be liked which prevents us from taking a hard line, or we seek to avoid confrontation and therefore avoid those awkward conversations you sometimes need to have with staff, or whether you simply do not have the confidence to stand out in front – leadership is tough.

From the moment you agreed to become a partner however you agreed to become a leader – tough or not.

We are unusual in that law firms, like accountants, historically have not just had one leader, as you would have in a company, but all partners or members are leaders – irrespective of whether one person is notionally nominated to lead.

Be a good leader

As owners it is therefore easy to fall into the trap that because we are owners we do not have to toe the line, we do not have to do what has been agreed, even though we agreed it. After all, that applies to the staff and we are not staff.

Somehow as owners we are different to the staff and different rules apply to us. We make the rules for the staff but after that we do what we want. And as there may be quite a few of the "what we want" as a business you can end up with a multitude of different approaches all the while telling the staff they must do things in a certain way.

Then as owners we are surprised why staff do not comply with our directives and also do their own thing. We complain that our staff just do not do as we ask.

Small wonder since we do not set the example.

Worse still is where some partners positively undermine decisions taken and seek to sabotage them and their implementation. What should staff make of that?

Firstly, that the decision is not important and therefore can be ignored.

Secondly, that there is clear disagreement within the partnership and therefore like children seeking to play one parent off against the other, staff will play the partners off against each other. It is human nature.

Have cabinet responsibility

Cabinet responsibility is a key element of good leadership. We see how damaging it is to political parties. Why think it is any less damaging to your business?

It is important to accept that as a group you will not agree on everything and that there will be decisions you as individuals will have to implement which you do not agree with. However you have been through your process and have debated the issue. You have had your say. A decision has been made. Like it or not for the benefit of the business you now need to support that decision and support its implementation.

Of course if there is too much disagreement within the partnership then you may face a much larger question – is the partnership working? Should you be in partnership together? Major disagreements on too many aspects of your business may mean you are not aligned and that you need to work on your alignment and find agreement or part ways.

Keep disagreements in the board room

Whatever the disagreements keep them in the board room. Don't let on to your staff. It will make them nervous and will make it much harder to bring unity within your business.

Make decisions

Good leaders need to be decisive. By all means take time to reach your decision (although not too long) but decisions have to be made. Too often I encountered an unwillingness to reach a decision. The thing about decisions is that they can be hard to make because you simply do not know which is the best way to go. However at the end of the day you can only do your best based on the information you have. There is no right and wrong. Usually there is a good or better decision. Occasionally a bad decision. Few will however be irreversible or fatal. As circumstances change revise your decisions or develop them. Sitting on the fence however should rarely be an option and if it is it should be because you have made a conscious decision that it is the best option at that time – in other words you have made a decision.

I recall in the early 2000s when the economy took a downward turn not as badly as in 2008 but nevertheless enough to impact significantly on the firm's financial performance. For 5 months we made little profit and barely covered overheads. There were no signs of things improving in the immediate future. Each month we decided to see how the next month went. In reality we were simply putting off making any decision. We did not want to take the steps we clearly needed to. In the sixth month of making no profit I asked the question "what are we waiting for?", "are we waiting for the day we make a loss before taking steps?" "should we not take control before we make a loss?"

I recall that the management team had been sitting there for hours discussing what to do and it was very late. We decided to leave it for another month. I was very unhappy with that conclusion. It was another month's "cop out". I remained seated and asked the questions.

It took us about 10 minutes to agree that we needed to take action.

Take control

Decisions are about taking control in a way and at time of your choosing. Being forced to make decisions with a gun to your head are rarely good circumstances for good decisions.

By deciding that we had to take steps to improve the financial performance we were forced to take a good look at how efficiently we were operating and what changes were needed. We found there had been an element of job creation making us quite simply inefficient. Redundancies on that occasion was the answer, in addition to a variety of operational changes. Not only did our financial performance improve, so did our overall efficiency. I am not convinced we would have made the best overall decisions had we been making them in a "panic" situation triggered by a financial loss.

Bear in mind that putting off decisions rarely avoids the issue. In the end you will probably need to make some decision or take action. The question is whether you do so when you have options or when circumstances are forcing you and whether because of this your options have become more limited.

Leadership is not a popularity contest

We all like to be liked. The reality is however that as a leader you will not be liked by everyone. Not only is this because not everyone will like you (do you know anyone who is universally liked?) but because people will not like your decisions and therefore not like you for making them.

Your staff will look at your decisions from their own perspective and whether it works for them rather than the firm as a whole. The statement "you can't please all of the people all of the time" is so true. A decision will be great for some and not so good for others.

As a leader you need to accept this and being popular unfortunately should not be your driving force. Aim for respect rather than being popular. You can respect someone you do not like.

Base your decision on what is best for the long term future of the firm and the staff, not on trying to please your staff. Reach those decisions applying principles of fairness and reasonableness and apply consistency to them. Ensure you can explain the decisions and the reasons for them. Even the most disgruntled of people cannot argue with decisions based on these principles – although that is not to say they will not try!

Implement your decisions

Decisions sadly don't implement themselves. They need to be carried through to their conclusion or implemented and adhered to. This is where so many businesses fail and law firms are top of the list.

We have decided that all letters must be answered within 3 days. We are promoting this on our website. No one adheres to it and eventually you remove it from your literature since it is not true. It is an embarrassing failure and as leaders you will have lost respect.

Assuming that your objectives are realistic and good for the business, having set them, as leaders set the example and then ensure that staff comply. Compliance needs to be universal. Exceptions should not apply. Either the requirements you have set are reasonable and beneficial overall or they are not. If they are not or do not work reverse them. However ensure it is your decision to reverse them not the staff. If you are going to be successful your team needs to work in unison and in accordance with the practices you have set. By all means consult with the staff but you make the final decision and you should expect compliance.

Be clear about what the consequences of non compliance are and ensure that you follow up. Good leaders are not afraid to do what they say. You have been warned and I mean what I say!

Human beings despite our huge talent for innovation and creativity also need boundaries. As children when we are told not to do something we do precisely that. I was told as a child not to touch the coals in the fire as they would hurt me. What did I do – picked up a coal and burnt my hand. I never did it again!

When you train dogs, consistency of commands and actions is key to ensuring they learn to obey. Your consistency shows that you mean what you say and your dog learns to understand this and therefore complies. As soon as they realise you don't mean it they ignore you.

As people we are not that different to dogs! If we think we can get away with not doing something despite being asked to, we do, particularly if it does not suit us. We also know instinctively with whom we can get away with it and where we can't. Our German Shepherd, Duke knows exactly what he can get away with and where he has to toe the line. Unfortunately we are poor pack leaders and he gets away with far more than he should!

Be a leader where people know you mean what you say. It creates better team work and a clearer understanding of what you expect of your staff and what they can expect from you.

Leaders have responsibility

My final comment on being a leader is that you carry a lot of responsibility. You are responsible for your staff. They depend on you. Their jobs depend on you. If you run a successful firm their jobs are secure. They have limited control over this.

You are responsible for making sure it works. This includes dealing with any disruptive influences.

Too often I heard the phrase "I do not like confrontation". Discussions with staff do not have to be confrontational and indeed in most cases they are not. The member of staff who is persistently late needs to be spoken to. It sets a bad example for everyone else unless it is acceptable for everyone to be late and arrive when they want. But it does not have to be a confrontational conversation. Explaining why it is not acceptable to be late and how it impacts on the rest of the firm should be enough. You are having a conversation. If it leads to a confrontation either you have a difficult member of staff or maybe you are not approaching it in the right way.

We had a member of staff who was about 15 minutes late every day. I asked the partner in charge of the department to have a word. They came back and explained that the reason the staff member was late was because the train they caught came in at 9am and they then had to walk to the office. It almost made sense, before I gave it more thought. Take an earlier train was my eventual response.

There are countless books on leadership. It is a complex issue but in the end it is about taking charge, not only being seen to be in charge but actually being in charge. Making decisions, however hard, when they need to be taken. Setting the example, being there to help and support your teams, and guiding the business along the planned path. It is about taking your responsibilities seriously. You are responsible for the livelihood of your staff. They have a right to expect leadership from you.

CHAPTER SIX
THE NO NONSENSE CHICKEN
AMONG THE FOXES

As with all of the thoughts I have covered, there are countless books on marketing and promoting your business. Before embarking on writing this chapter I wondered what I could add from my own experience. One thing – it is trial and error. Not everything works and the biggest trap you can fall into is that you waste a lot of money on doing things that make you feel like you are doing **something** but in reality you are not and instead are just fooling yourself.

Stick to what you know

I recall watching a programme on TV about the German company which makes the HB pencils. They were asked why over so many generations they had (as a family business) remained so successful. Their answer was that they had stuck to what they were good at – making pencils. It seemed extraordinary to me that in a world that is changing and has changed so dramatically over the last 100 years a business can do well with a product which it started to manufacture a long time ago. It was clear however that time had not passed them by and they had adapted to new technology and processes. At the end of the day however it was the quality of their product, their knowledge and experience gained over many years and their ability to adapt to modern technology which had ensured their survival.

It reinforced what I have learnt, namely that delivering a good service remains the best marketing tool you can have. There is no substitute for recommendations and conversely there is no worse damage than bad recommendations.

That is not to say you do not need to get your name out there. You do. I deliberately do not use the word brand. I came across a number of consultants who tried to persuade me that we were building a brand. I have come across numerous small businesses who talk in terms of building a brand. It is of course possible but in reality for an average law firm to build a brand is nigh on impossible. The level of expenditure that would be needed is unaffordable to most if not all law firms. Indeed the point is regularly made in Dragons Den when they talk about developing a brand.

A true brand requires a USP (unique selling point) and law firms generally really struggle to develop one unless they are niche. Without a clear USP how can you develop a brand? If quality of service is your USP – wake up. Quality is the USP of hundreds of law firms. It's hardly unique.

Unless you are international your average law firm should work at building a good reputation. Marketing can help but **delivery** of what you say you offer is key.

<u>Who is your marketing team?</u>

And when one talks about marketing what do you mean? There was a time when marketing people drew a distinction between marketing and business development. You were encouraged to employ both on the basis that the skill base was different. I was never able to reconcile myself to this. If marketing is not about business development and business development did not require marketing how did this work? I used to insist that one person must be able to do both. These days the distinction does not exist in the same way and people are expected to have all the skills.

You market to get your name out there and as a result to bring in more business. Marketing and business development are synonymous.

Where the real change, I believe has occurred when it comes to marketing, is with the advent of technology. And therein lies a major challenge.

I should probably not say this let alone write it but when it comes to technology age can play a part in terms of one's knowledge and ability to use it and therefore the planning of how to use it in your business.

I am talking here about you as a lawyer and partner in your firm rather than someone who works in IT and I apologise to all those who feel offended by this.

Like most firms we used to have a marketing manager (who by definition was a bit older with experience in marketing) and an assistant. Although some aspects were carried out well there was a lot that always seemed to be lacking when it came to the overall business development and new ways of promoting the firm.

Normal spreadsheets were the norm to use and we found ourselves repeating much of what we had done in previous years. In principle there was nothing wrong with that but I always felt we should be doing more given how technology was moving on and the way the new generation were communicating with each other. I simply did not know how or in what way. I was even then a partial dinosaur when it came to new technology. I recognised however that I was a dinosaur and that there was a world out there that we needed to include.

It was when we found ourselves in a situation without a marketing department that it gave us the opportunity to rethink its makeup and how it could work. It occurred to me that our marketing took two forms. One was events of which we did quite a lot. The other was digital marketing – whether this was use of Twitter, LinkedIn, Facebook, email promotion, better use of a CRM system, mobile phone messages, Instagram etc.

I realised that, like me, marketing managers with experience did not appear to have the knowledge or skills to properly make use of these new media. They also tended to be a little out of date. The young seem to be born with this knowledge and are keen to use anything new. If you can't work your DVD get a 5 year old to have a look. How they know it is beyond me but we all know they do.

I would not be able to count how many partners I spoke to who said they did not understand Facebook did not want to use it, couldn't see the point, didn't trust it – the justifications went on.

In any event, I concluded that it would be worth trying to recruit an event manager and what I described as a digital marketing person. The experiment worked really well. The event manager carried on with the kind of things that we had been doing previously but the digital marketing manager not only worked our CRM system better than ever before but was able to help with design of brochures, build better use of digital marketing media and pushed us forward, albeit slowly, to more online promotion. One must remember these are lawyers we are dealing with who do not move at the fastest pace!

It was a very effective experiment and the lesson learnt is take time out to review the make up of your marketing team. Have you got the right skills given the fast development of technology and ways of doing things and given the kind of marketing you want to do. Do you have the skills to help you look forward as to what might be effective in the next few years?

Whatever anyone tells you, marketing is about trial and error. Some things will work for one business and not another and vice versa. Why is anybody's guess – maybe it is just a matter of timing.

Have clear objectives and monitor

Having said that I believe there are still some old fashioned principles which still apply even in this age of technology.

Be clear about what you want to achieve. Is it name aware-ness (I stay away from brand awareness) or are you seeking new clients as a result of the initiative. Although the overall objective is of course always the latter, some events can generate leads and others primarily simply get your business name out there.

How are you going to measure whether it is effective? This is possibly the hardest thing to do but however hard it is do not ignore the requirement to consider effectiveness. Sometimes it might be only hearing how others speak about your event and its success, others might involve whether you actually generate new work. Not carrying out a review simply means you are working blind and following a path and incurring cost without any assessment of whether it is worthwhile.

If you don't think something is working or the cost benefit analysis is not right, stop. Rethink and follow different approaches. I don't believe there is any such thing as a marketing failure. There is only some that work better than others. The trick is to work out what is working better and what is not. The fact that it might be hard is no reason not to try and assess and to do so at all times.

Advertising in magazines is a classic example of it being hard to assess whether it is working. We advertised (I have to say for not great expense) in a local publication for many years. We never generated work that we could identify. We felt however that it did get the name out in the local area and this was the main objective. After a few years we stopped as we felt that the name awareness had probably been achieved and we were not getting any further benefit. There was no way of knowing for sure but we had to take best guesses and make decisions based on that.

I often heard people say that they had tried something and it had not worked and therefore should not be tried again. That might be right but bear in mind what did not work 3 years ago might work now. Times change, moods change. I would suggest always rethinking all options and reviewing why something might not have worked previously. If you are satisfied it would not work now, fine, just be prepared to challenge any previous perceptions of failure.

Keep your message simple

Keep your marketing language simple and jargon free. "So you get the justice you deserve" is a jargon slogan I have come to loath. "Exceptional service" is another. Used to death by the service industry. It doesn't actually mean anything and simply does not speak to the client.

Ask your clients what they want

Whether other industries are the same I can't say, but lawyers seem to believe that they know what their clients want to hear and are looking for. We seem to rarely ask them and when we do we tend to ignore what we are told. If all your clients comment on how expensive you are or lawyers are then why as a profession do we not address this in our marketing. For example is charging £1000 for a conveyance expensive when you can pay £500 for a washing machine?

Buying a house involves the most expensive purchase of your life and one, you hope, will support you (whether you buy and sell later) for the rest of your life. Your washing machine might have a life span of 5 years and is a depreciating asset.

We need to explain to our clients far more the value we bring if cost is a main issue (which if we are honest we know it is). We talk about value for money but even that means different things to different people and what does it really mean?

If your clients say they are worried about meeting their solicitor (and many people are – a bit like going to the dentist) why not address this and tackle such a concern. Instead we go on about delivering exceptional service or quality service when as a client this is taken as read (afterall who chooses to use someone who does not do a good job).

I recall a meeting with our bankers at a time I was looking to change banks. I had over the years had many conversations with them about building the relationship, about cross referral of work and what we were looking for from our bankers. It had fallen on deaf ears or they had not taken my indication that we would move banks seriously. In any event their response to me during a "last chance for them" conversation was to say they were very good at banking! It was said in all seriousness but I had to laugh. I told them that if they were not good at their core business then they should shut up shop. I took it as given that they could offer good banking services. That was not however something extra, and it was the extra we were looking for.

Clients expect us to know the law and expect us to be able to offer good legal advice. It is what else we offer that matters and it is the extra that is the differentiator amongst law firms.

When we look at our messages we rarely seem to tackle the issues which really concern our clients – instead we tell them what we think they should know and what we want them to hear. Our communication with our clients is generally very poor.

There is now technology which enables you to obtain information about what the "chatter" is in your industry. It spans all social media and analyses conversations that are being had about a particular topic or news. Although expensive to obtain it can be very useful when deciding on your marketing strategy. I suppose in some ways it has replaced street questionnaires and is far more sophisticated. The general principle however has not changed. It is about hearing what the consumer is saying and thinking and using that to talk to them through your marketing initiatives.

Use technology wisely

Technology is wonderful in so many ways. It has made life a lot easier in so many ways. I still recall the nightmare of mistakes in letters and having to have them retyped. I used to feel for secretaries and at the same time clients had to wait so much longer for their letters! I recall having to carefully amend mistakes in letters with the white Tipp-Ex sheet. A time consuming and messy exercise. Now we just delete on screen – and that is just the start of how helpful technology is, and can be.

However it is a tool not the master. My mantra was always that technology is there to help not rule. If technology does not offer the best way of doing something then do it differently, even if that means the old fashioned way. Sometimes old fashioned methods can still work best. And this applies to how you use technology for marketing.

It's about the real person

Remember that there are real people on the other end. It is easy to think that a marketing email is a substitute for a conversation. The over use of emails is extraordinary. We are so submerged by them that we hardly read them. Nevertheless many businesses believe that if we are bombarded enough maybe something will stick.

Always remember that you are looking to connect with real people. Despite technology there can be no substitute for human contact and human interaction.

Which might explain why networking events still have a large place in any business' marketing plan. An opportunity to meet new people (well lawyers, accountants and bankers at least) and to talk to people. The concept is good unless you are the unfortunate actual business person amongst the hoards of lawyers, accountants and bankers! Those poor individuals find themselves set upon because they are such a rare phenomenon. Contacts are always good.

Not everyone is good at marketing

Not everyone however is good at networking and building contacts. It requires skill and follow through. Too many lawyers see networking as a chore and one to be ticked off the list. For those with that approach it is a complete waste of their time and the firm's money. If attending networking events is part of your marketing strategy get the right people there. Consider attending less events but with the right people attending. Once again monitor and evaluate effectiveness and follow up. Was the event worthwhile, who did you meet, what follow up was agreed and has this been actioned are all questions that should form part of your overall marketing evaluation.

Don't forget your existing clients

It is easy to forget your existing clients in one's enthusiasm for getting out there for new clients. However, bear in mind it is much harder to get new clients on board than it is to generate more work from your existing clients – whether directly from them or through their recommendations. Your existing clients already like you otherwise they wouldn't be your clients. They are likely to stay with you provided you get the care right. Of course you will lose some (they go elsewhere, move away from the area, etc) and it is those that you are really looking to replace. However consider what proportion of effort you put in to getting new clients versus looking after your existing clients. Like most law firms I suspect you will find that most of your budget is spent on seeking new clients. It is the opposite of what we should do. It is much easier to look after existing clients and encourage them to recommend or give you more work than it is to generate new ones.

Marketing is not something someone else can do for you. Whereas some aspects can be outsourced in the end it is about your firm, who you are and how you get your message out there. Only you can really do it. It is about touching base with the clients you act for now and the clients you want to act for in the future.

It is not an exact science. There is a large element of hit and miss. It is about being innovative and making sure you understand how the people you want to reach want to be contacted and approached. It is about letting the outside world see who you are and what you have to offer. We are a people industry. We can say what we like but it is about how we come across as people that matters in the end.

CHAPTER SEVEN
NO NONSENSE IT'S
YOUR HERD

I started this book with listening to your gut and I conclude it with your people. Managing your staff is likely to be your biggest challenge. It feels trite to say, but they really are at the heart of what you do. They make or break your business. In the end it all comes together with them and it falls apart with them. As a service industry, it is how good your staff perform which ultimately determines how well you do.

We are not that different

Although human beings pride themselves on being different I would at one level challenge this. I believe (and I admit this is at a very elementary level of psychology) we all have the same fundamental needs. What makes us different is the level of importance each of those fundamental needs have for each of us.

For example, for some, security is more important than for others but it would be an unusual person who needs no security at all. We all like to be liked but some have a greater need to be liked than others. For some, money is the main driver, for others money is less important and their driver may be helping others or job satisfaction. Few want to earn no money at all. Even someone driven only by money must enjoy their work at some level.

Some seek control or responsibility but to suggest that there are some people who are content with no control over their daily lives or who seek no responsibility at all would be surprising. Different people simply seek different levels of control or responsibility.

I could go on about all our various characteristics but the point I am seeking to make is that human make up is not that different within the work place – it is the strength of each of the elements which varies.

However, I do believe there are a few fundamental ingredients, which although old fashioned, still hold good when it comes to treating and managing your staff.

Respect each other, work together as a team and involve your staff

A firm where everyone truly treats each other with respect, works as a team and is involved in the business at some level will be a very successful firm.

I have often heard businesses talk about how everyone respects each other. I have rarely seen it in reality. Whether it is secretaries who belittle the office managers, senior lawyers belittling trainees or junior staff or partners undermining each other or the staff, a lack of respect amongst each other is far more common than is admitted. I also think and fear this is a growing trend in the world generally. We all appear to be showing each other less respect in all walks of life. Naturally this will translate itself into how we conduct ourselves in our working lives.

This is a great shame since it does not take much to show respect, indeed it costs nothing, but can have a huge impact on a business' performance, staff morale and its overall success.

In part it comes back to leadership and how partners behave. Set the example and your staff will follow. Allow bad behaviour to go unchallenged and your staff will do as they wish.

Without respect it is hard to achieve teamwork. Good teamwork starts with respect for each member of the team and in this context the team is the whole firm not a department, a team of lawyer/secretary or any other smaller team within the firm. I would challenge anyone to argue that good teamwork is not the secret to success. Football teams win when they work as a team. Any lack of teamwork by one player alone spells almost certain defeat on the football pitch.

And finally if you involve your staff, tell them your plans and seek their views they will engage with you. They will have an interest in the success of the plans. Further, not only are you showing them respect by asking for their views, you are also telling them you value their opinion. You may also be surprised by the good ideas they can contribute. Better still they can help you not only formulate your plans but implement them. Understanding why you are doing something is half the battle to getting it done. It is also half the battle to working as a team in which each player knows their part, its relevance and importance.

I am not suggesting that respect, teamwork and involvement are the only criteria to success and managing your staff effectively. This is something consultants love to talk about as the culture of a firm, core values and ethos.

Be clear about your firm's ethos

Whatever terminology you choose to give it, in the end you need to identify and decide what the characteristics of your firm are. When you are looking to recruit, apart from the job skills, what characteristics are you looking for? Are you a firm where everyone is driven by money at any cost (possibly even at the expense of the client)? If so you will need to recruit individuals who can thrive and work in that environment.

If your objective is client care and service delivery then a culture of "money for me" above all else is unlikely to ensure that clients are put first.

There is no right and wrong as to a business characteristic. Where it does go wrong is if a business says it is one thing but is in fact something completely different or it has no real characteristic at all and is made up of staff who have very different objectives at heart. In that case there is no common bond. It will make recruitment a nightmare for you (what kind of person should you be looking for?) and will make it hard to achieve your goals. You will find that everyone is pulling in different directions.

It is only if you really understand who and what you really are as opposed to just saying it (or perhaps wanting to believe it even if you know it isn't true) that you will be able to build a business with a true characteristic or ethos. You will understand the type of people you should be looking to recruit, they are more likely to fit and get on, teamwork will develop and goals can be achieved.

Get the right people on board

"You can teach someone the necessary skills for the job but you cannot change their characteristics" was something an HR manager once told me and how true is that? Getting the people with the right characteristics for your firm is far more important than the best skills. If you can do both great, but if you have to choose, look at the characteristics first.

Recruitment is an art not a science and with the best will in the world you will sometimes get it wrong. Some people simply will not fit into your firm even with the right characteristics. However having a clear understanding of the type of person who should fit into your organisation will reduce how often you get it wrong. Getting it wrong can be so damaging and expensive in so many ways.

I have never understood how a strong team can nevertheless be destroyed by one disruptive person. You would think that the team would be stronger than the solo dissident and that they would make short sharp shrift of the rogue team player. But in my experience that does not seem to be what happens. It is a bit of a phenomenon but sadly true.

Therefore, if faced with someone who does not fit in, deal with it. Do not allow it to drag on. Some people will just not fit in. It does not make them a bad person or you a bad employer. It happens and it is usually best for both parties to part. Recognise this and recognise it early before too much damage is done.

Demand compliance

Adhering to the characteristics of your firm needs to be more important than anything else. Your staff must play by your rules and expectations. That includes good financial performers.

Beware of the good financial performer who believes they have immunity – immunity from complying with the firm's philosophy; who believes they are entitled to be disruptive or not to toe the line.

Despite their good financial performance consider to what extent they affect the performance of your other staff? How much money are you losing through the disruptive or non compliant behaviour of your good performer from your other staff? Are your staff becoming dissatisfied, is resentment building up, are staff leaving because they don't understand why you won't deal with someone who clearly does not follow the business expectations?

There are countless ways your business could be losing money despite Mr/Ms disruptive bringing in good fees. It is hidden but don't underestimate the loss you might be making. Those who do not act in line with your expectations and the characteristics you are looking for should not remain with you – no matter how much money they bring in.

Try delegation

Lawyers do have a tendency to be poor delegators and often this is at the heart of not passing on responsibility to your staff. Try it!

It can ease your burden of work and often your staff will do a better job. Be prepared to give responsibility and freedom to carry it out but manage any abuse of that freedom. Set the standards and make sure people meet them. If they are wrong change them, don't ignore them.

Ignoring non compliance means the rules are not important so everyone can ignore them. You set the standard or process for a reason and not to make life difficult. Manage compliance and show your staff that they can rely on you to ensure everyone meets the standards. Otherwise it will always not be fair to some and there is no easier way of upsetting your workforce than by not treating them fairly.

By delegating you may find that your staff will be more willing to comply with your expectations. By giving them more responsibility you may find that they become the game keeper as opposed to the poacher!

Tackle underperformers

If there is one thing we hate to do it is to tackle underperformance particularly if there is a good reason for the underperformance or so it seems. Very occasionally there is a good reason for failing to meet the targets set but actually that should be rare. Your staff will watch you to see if you are dealing with underperformance. If you don't they will see you as weak and will stop trying to do their best. Why should they? There are no consequences.

You will find it hard to retain good people if you are even able to recruit them in the first place. Your work force will be unhappy. Staff turnaround will increase creating a destabilising effect. What you will be left with are second rate performers. It will happen slowly so you might not even realise it. But it will happen. All because you did not tackle the people who were not pulling their weight.

It is a tough thing to do and I don't need to spell it out that employment laws need to be followed at all times but avoiding tackling underperformers is likely to simply make the situation worse as time goes by. It rarely sorts itself out.

I hate bonuses

I cannot leave this topic without touching on bonuses. It is a matter for each business to consider but my view reinforced over the years is that they are destructive and unhealthy for a business. It seems to me it is better to pay your good people well and let them deliver a good service to your clients without any self interest being involved.

Experience showed me that as soon as bonuses were involved shortcuts were taken in order to achieve the target needed. Client care went out of the window and so did teamwork. Why would anyone help someone else if they get no credit for it, particularly when they could spend the time doing work for which they would get credit?

There is no bonus scheme I ever came across which covered all bases, was truly workable, objective and fair.

Indeed, years ago when it was introduced in a large accountancy practice they explained to me in great detail how it worked. The partner explained that he would be assessed by a set group of partners. "Who assessed those partners" I asked? "Another team of partners"." Who assessed those partners" I asked? "The management board". "Who assessed the management board?"" The senior partner and managing partner." "Who assessed the senior partner and the managing partner?" I asked? "Ah no one" was the answer. "Well that can't be right" I said. "Surely to be fair their performance must also be assessed?"

And let's face it, if the assessment is a circular assessment won't I assess you well on the basis you reciprocate and we all get our bonuses?

I met the same partner many years later. He had left the accountancy firm. He was unimpressed with how bonuses had worked – or not worked. It was a shame since he had been so enthusiastic about it when it was introduced.

If we have not learnt our lessons from the banking crisis and from countless scandals about mis-sold products when will we? It is human nature to put ourselves and our own interests first ahead of anything else and for many to go down a less than straight path if we individually can make more money or benefit more as a result.

I recall when we took over a team of lawyers there was one who outperformed everyone else in the department. They achieved in 4 days what others were unable to do in 5. I either wanted to clone them or dismiss them. A review of their files showed that shortcuts were taken which could have resulted in large negligence claims. The targets were however achieved and a bonus became payable. We avoided negligence claims and parted ways.

Even a bonus based on the performance of the firm has its flaws. Why would everyone get a bonus if they have not achieved their target even though the firm has achieved its target but through the over performance of some. An approach which on the face of it might seem fairer runs the risk of upsetting your good performers who see underperformers getting the same as them for underperformance.

Bonuses to my mind feed our worst characteristics.

That is not to say that there are not huge pressures on businesses to offer bonuses and I understand the dilemma. If you decide to go down the route expect dissatisfaction over time from some of your teams and a lot of "why did they get it when I have done some much more", "my assessment is not fair", "my manager does not like me"," they got a bonus but they never do anything in addition" – the backchat will go on. My advice remains – pay your staff well and then ask them to work hard.

Team – Together Everyone Achieves More

A good team can be a joy to work with. You can achieve unbelievable results if you work well together. Your staff at the end of the day depend on you for their well being. Manage them well and you and they will be rewarded. Sounds easy but we all know it isn't.

Bear in mind that people fundamentally want to be treated fairly in all respects. We want to feel valued and recognised. We want to be able to live at the least comfortably. We want to have a balance in life. Work towards all of this and your staff are likely to be there for you and work with you to achieve your objectives. No one comes to work to do a bad job and this is always a good starting point.

CHAPTER EIGHT
NO NONSENSE AND FINALLY...

It's just common sense.

By all means read the countless books written on how to manage your business and your staff. There are good messages in all of them and some words of wisdom which if applied well can make a difference. But be careful not to get too caught up in the theory and miss reality. It is easy to overcomplicate approaches and miss the simple but often effective answers.

By all means engage consultants to help but be wary of their theories and promises. They often do not stack up. They often do not have the real experience needed to help you. Select getting help carefully.

Be a leader and show proper leadership. Give your staff confidence in you.

Work as a team – it is much more fun.

Be honest and upfront in your dealings with your clients and your staff. A lack of reality is easily spotted.

Be cautious but not too cautious that you never get anything done.

Be prepared to take risks but always look at all aspects of the risks and make informed decisions.

Manage your money sensibly but be prepared to take calculated risks when it comes to investments.

Be fair and loyal to your staff and treat them with respect. Remember we are all just people.

Have your clear plan and live it. Don't let it gather dust.

Re-evaluate everything you do.

Above all keep your integrity – even if those around you do not.

How hard can it be? Good luck!

ABOUT THE AUTHOR

After studying law at Warwick University Bettina spent a few months working at the European Patent Office in Munich before qualifying as a solicitor in 1989.

She was made a partner soon after qualifying, which brought with it, not just building legal know-how, but the additional responsibilities of running a firm, managing staff and developing a business.

At the age of 39 she was appointed managing partner responsible for all aspects of managing the firm. Known for her clear thinking, quick ability to analyse situations together with a no nonsense style of management, Bettina steered her firm through the toughest recession of our generation while still maintaining the firm's strategy for growth. Her skills and efforts were rewarded when she was named Lawnet Managing Partner of the Year in 2009.

Despite having little time for academic consultants, she offers consulting services to businesses who welcome someone who has 30 years genuine experience in business, who understands the real issues they face but who does not believe in "consultant speak."

Also a keen traveller, Bettina has backpacked around many parts of the world, considered an unusual way to travel by some. Bettina enjoys learning about new cultures and ways of life. She says "Backpacking gives you a slightly greater insight into a country than with an organised tour. I like to try to get at the heart of a country and its people. Travel has the ability to really broaden your horizons in so many ways."

Resource7 Ltd
www.resource7.co.uk
bettina@resource7.co.uk
07544 528 296

TenBroeke Co
www.tenbroekeco.com
bettina.brueggemann@tenbroekco.com
07544 528 296

TenBroeke Co
Transforming Infrastructure Delivery

MORE BOOKS BY
LAW BRIEF PUBLISHING

'Ellis and Kevan on Credit Hire, 5th Edition' by Aidan Ellis & Tim Kevan
'RTA Allegations of Fraud in a Post-Jackson Era: The Handbook, 2nd Edition' by Andrew Mckie
'A Practical Guide to Holiday Sickness Claims' by Andrew Mckie & Ian Skeate
'RTA Personal Injury Claims: A Practical Guide Post-Jackson' by Andrew Mckie
'On Experts: CPR35 for Lawyers and Experts' by David Boyle
'A Practical Guide to Claims Arising From Accidents Abroad and Travel Claims' by Andrew Mckie & Ian Skeate
'A Practical Guide to Claims Arising from Fatal Accidents' by James Patience
'A Practical Approach to Clinical Negligence Post-Jackson' by Geoffrey Simpson-Scott
'A Practical Guide to Personal Injury Trusts' by Alan Robinson
'Occupiers, Highways and Defective Premises Claims: A Practical Guide Post-Jackson' by Andrew Mckie
'Employers' Liability Claims: A Practical Guide Post-Jackson' by Andrew Mckie
'A Practical Guide to Subtle Brain Injury Claims' by Pankaj Madan
'The Law of Driverless Cars: An Introduction' by Alex Glassbrook

'A Practical Guide to Costs in Personal Injury Cases' by Matthew Hoe
'A Practical Guide to Alternative Dispute Resolution in Personal Injury Claims – Getting the Most Out of ADR Post-Jackson' by Peter Causton, Nichola Evans, James Arrowsmith
'A Practical Guide to Personal Injuries in Sport' by Adam Walker & Patricia Leonard
'A Practical Guide to Marketing for Lawyers' by Catherine Bailey & Jennet Ingram
'Baby Steps: A Guide to Maternity Leave and Maternity Pay' by Leah Waller
'The Queen's Counsel Lawyer's Omnibus: 20 Years of Cartoons from the Times 1993-2013' by Alex Steuart Williams

These books and more are available to order online direct from the publisher at www.lawbriefpublishing.com, where you can also read free sample chapters. For any queries, contact us on 0844 587 2383 or mail@lawbriefpublishing. com.

Our books are also usually in stock at www.amazon.co.uk with free next day delivery for Prime members, and at good legal bookshops such as Hammicks and Wildy & Sons.

We are regularly launching new books in our series of practical day-to-day practitioners' guides. Visit our website and join our free newsletter to be kept informed.

Lightning Source UK Ltd.
Milton Keynes UK
UKOW01f1001071017
310545UK00004B/184/P

9 781911 035251